The Way I Feel Too

Written and Illustrated by
Janan Cain

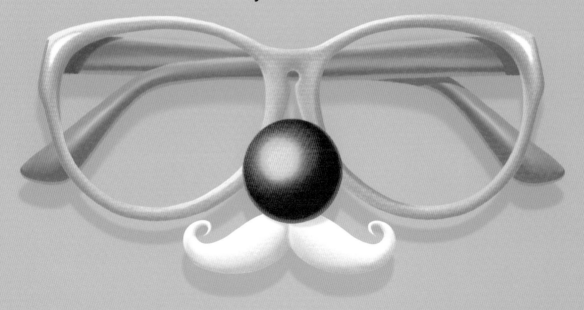

CHICAGO

Copyright © 2023 by Janan Cain
All rights reserved.

Published by Parenting Press
An imprint of Chicago Review Press Incorporated
814 North Franklin Street
Chicago, Illinois 60610

ISBN 978-1-64160-986-9
Library of Congress Cataloging-in-Publication Data
Is available from the Library of Congress.

Illustrations rendered in Procreate on an iPad
Verses rendered in Adobe Illustrator and Procreate

Printed in China
5 4 3 2 1

This book is dedicated to my GREAT nieces and nephews—

Carter, Harper, Dean, Griffin, Archer, Collins, Margot, Eliza, Louie, and Levi

Love,
Aunt Janan

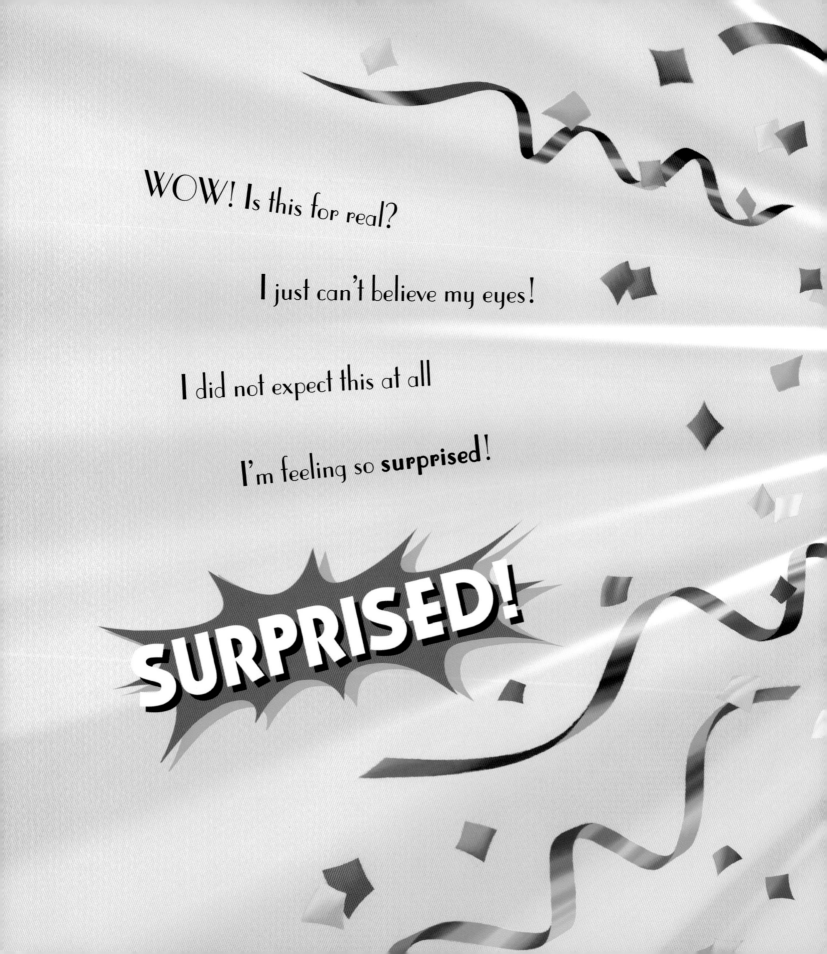

WOW! Is this for real?

I just can't believe my eyes!

I did not expect this at all

I'm feeling so **surprised**!

SURPRISED!

Lonely

I wish I were with all my friends

Having fun and laughing today.

Instead I feel **lonely** all by myself

I should ask a friend to play

Worried

My mind keeps thinking terrible thoughts

Of all the things that can go wrong.

I'm really **worried**, my stomach's in knots,

I want to feel calm and strong

I take a deep breath, then exhale my worries away.

My mind and body are **calm**, now everything will be okay

calm

CONFUSED

I just don't get it, I'm so **confused!**

It doesn't make sense to me.

Please be patient and explain it again,

I'll understand eventually

Disgusted

Ewwww!

Gross!

Yuck!

It smells like

stinky feet!

I feel

so **disgusted**

Get this thing

away from me!

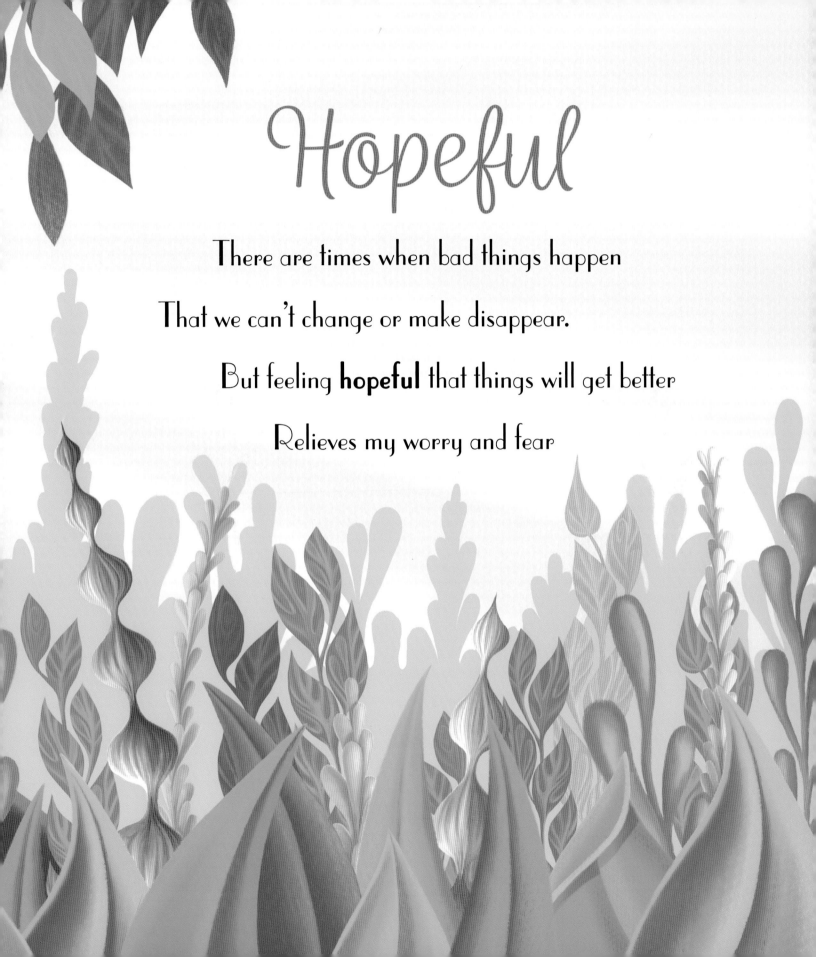

Hopeful

There are times when bad things happen

That we can't change or make disappear.

But feeling **hopeful** that things will get better

Relieves my worry and fear

Embarrassed

Everyone is

laughing at me.

I wish that I

could hide.

I'm **embarrassed**

as my face turns red,

I'm trying

not to cry

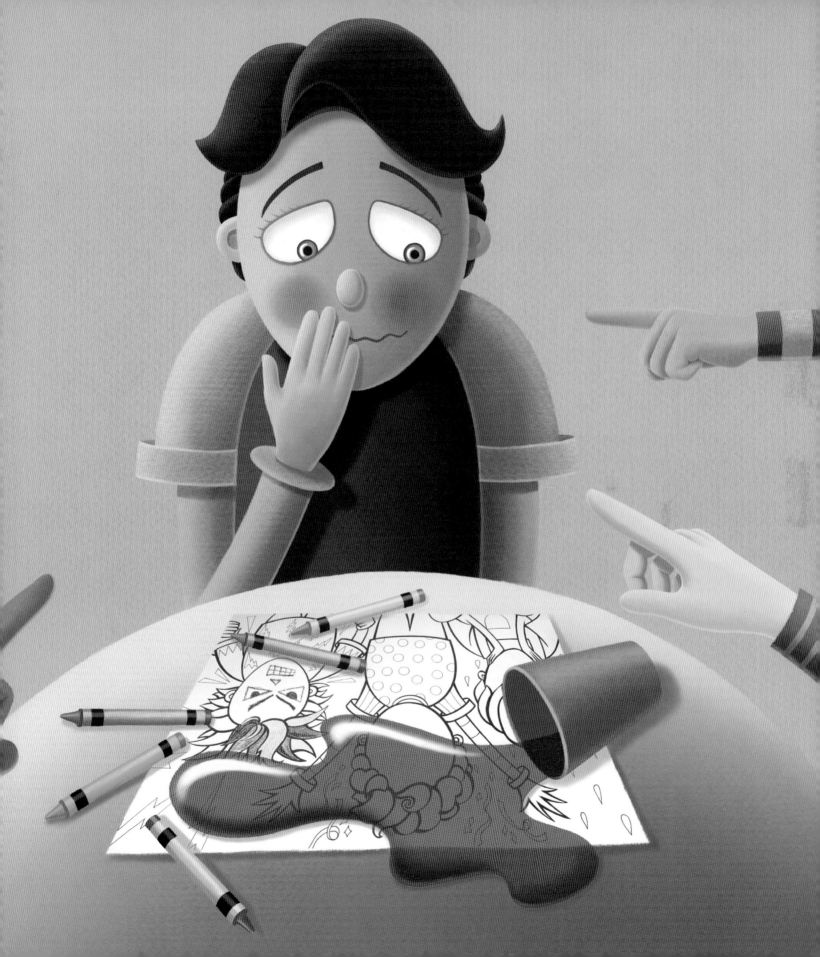

My nose is stuffy, my stomach hurts

My throat burns, so does my head

I can't play or do anything

I feel **sick** and need my bed

I know that I can do this!

I will give it all I've got!

I am feeling very **confident**

As I give it my best shot!

confident

When all I do is whine and frown

And try to pick a fight

It's not your fault, I just feel **grumpy**

Nothing seems quite right

Sorry

I can't stop thinking about the things I did

That made you cry and feel so bad.

The way I acted was very mean

I'm **sorry** I made you sad

loved

When I'm down you cheer me up

You know exactly what to do.

My heart is full, I feel so **loved**

When you hug me close to you

Lonely, grumpy, calm, or surprised
My feelings change throughout the day.
Tomorrow I'll have more feelings
Because they never go away!

We have learned that
emotional competence is essential for physical health.
Emotional competence (or emotional intelligence) is defined as
"an important set of personal and social skills for identifying,
interpreting and constructively responding to emotions in oneself and others."
If children learn to express themselves, they are less likely to experience anxiety and depression.

For that reason, I have created **The Way I Feel** and **The Way I Feel Too**
to teach children the language for their emotions.
I have two suggestions to parents while reading these books.
One, ask your child what circumstances made him or her feel happy, sad, jealous and so on.
Two, discuss how to deal with emotions.
Talk about what is okay to do or not okay to do as a reaction to their emotions.

Following are additional suggestions while reading this book to your children:

1) Explain to your child there is no such thing as a "bad" emotion. Negative feelings such as anger, fear, and anxiety are normal. Instead of disapproving or dismissing children's natural reactions give an example of a situation you experienced that made you feel a similar emotion. Ask your child what behavior is an acceptable way to cope with those negative feelings. Instead of telling your child not to hit their sibling, say "What can you do instead of hitting your sister?"

2) Teach your child various self-soothing techniques to help avoid emotional meltdowns, such as breathing exercises and meditation. Have him/her blow a tissue across the table. Or use bubbles to encourage a deep breath in and a careful, slow breath out.

—Janan Cain